Household
RECORD BOOK

PAINTINGS BY
MICHAEL EMMETT

EXLEY

First published in Great Britain in 1991 by Exley Publications Ltd.
Published simultaneously in 1992 by Exley Publications Ltd. in Great Britain, and
Exley Giftbooks in the USA.

Second printing, 1992

PAINTINGS BY MICHAEL EMMETT
EDITED BY HELEN EXLEY

Reproduced by permission of The Catto Gallery, Hampstead, London
– all rights reserved.

Designed by The Pinpoint Design Company

British Library Cataloguing in Publication Data available

ISBN 1-85015-270-5

Printed and bound in Spain by Grafo SA

*Also illustrated by Michael Emmett "Guest Book" – a beautiful book for
recording names and addresses of your visitors.*

Exley Publications Ltd, 16 Chalk Hill, Watford, Herts WD1 4BN, United Kingdom.
Exley Giftbooks, 359 East Main Street, Suite 3D, Mount Kisco, NY 10549, USA.

How to use this book

This book can help to revolutionize your life by giving you that most precious gift of all – time. How often have we all hunted for a record of the paint shade we chose for the bathroom only last year? And then gone to the hardware store and had to test all the pale blues to match it? And how many of us have busy lives interrupted by scrabbling around to take wallpaper measures that we took only three years ago but failed to make any notes of? Or tried to find the supplier of the special cloisonné repairer or shelf supplier we've always used? Or tried to remember details of the children's innoculations?

If you fill this book in, and update it, you will save those wasted hours.

The key word is "If". It's a quick job that needs regular small amounts of time – but time that will avoid *many* more hours of hassle and frustration rummaging around phone books and piles of paper. What's more, you won't *need* most of those piles of paper any more.

I've designed this book to be used whatever size of family or style of household you run. That's because I personally dislike record books that spell out endless pages of lists which don't apply to me and leave me four lines of space for a category that demands several pages.

For example, instead of having a small space headed "Electric Heater" (you probably have several, in which case you need much more space – or none, in which case you don't need the space at all!) I've suggested all possible categories at the top of each section and left you complete freedom to list the things *you* need to record.

Finally, three injunctions to make this book the revolution it could be:

1) Fill it in.

2) Keep adding to it.

3) Use it – and encourage everyone else in your home to use it.

Helen Exley

CONTENTS

Emergencies

Household Emergencies: This gives you space for telephone numbers and contact names of friends and relatives who could help with household crises.

Suggestions for you to list include burglar alarm company, credit card loss, doctor, electrician, glazier, hospital, keyholder, locksmith, plumber, school and work contact numbers.

_____
_____
_____
_____
_____
_____
_____
_____
_____
_____
_____
_____

WHERE TO FIND

**Emergency First Aid book
and medical supplies:**

**Main switch
to turn off electricity supply:**

**Stop cock
to turn off water supply:**

Annual Planner

This can be used for personal information – anniversaries, birthdays or travel arrangements, or reminders for yearly check-ups at the dentist, doctor or optician. You may also choose to add major regular items of annual expenditure – such as car or household insurance.

Annual Financial Planner

List your major items of expenditure in the left-hand column. Items could include Car Licence, Car Servicing and Repairs, Cleaning, Central Heating, Electricity, Gas, Holiday, Insurances, Water charges, and irregular, one-off major expenses.

This planner will enable you to budget for all your regular yearly expenses as well as making plans to finance any major unusual expense, like an expensive overseas tour or a house extension.

ITEM (Annual Totals)	YEAR	YEAR	YEAR	YEAR
RUNNING TOTALS				

ITEM (Annual Totals)	YEAR	YEAR	YEAR	YEAR
TOTALS BROUGHT FORWARD				
TOTALS FOR EACH YEAR				

Appliances

These pages can be used to note details of your purchase. Here is a checklist of suggested ideas: alarm, boiler, CD player, computer, dishwasher, electric blanket, electric drill, food processor, freezer, hobs, iron, lawn mower, microwave, radio, television, tumble drier, vacuum cleaner, video, washing machine, word processor.

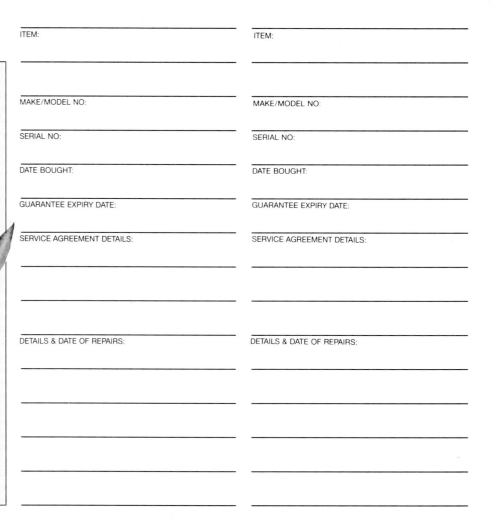

ITEM:

MAKE/MODEL NO:

SERIAL NO:

DATE BOUGHT:

GUARANTEE EXPIRY DATE:

SERVICE AGREEMENT DETAILS:

DETAILS & DATE OF REPAIRS:

ITEM:

MAKE/MODEL NO:

SERIAL NO:

DATE BOUGHT:

GUARANTEE EXPIRY DATE:

SERVICE AGREEMENT DETAILS:

DETAILS & DATE OF REPAIRS:

ITEM: | ITEM: | ITEM:

MAKE/MODEL NO: | MAKE/MODEL NO: | MAKE/MODEL NO:

SERIAL NO: | SERIAL NO: | SERIAL NO:

DATE BOUGHT: | DATE BOUGHT: | DATE BOUGHT:

GUARANTEE EXPIRY DATE: | GUARANTEE EXPIRY DATE: | GUARANTEE EXPIRY DATE:

SERVICE AGREEMENT DETAILS: | SERVICE AGREEMENT DETAILS: | SERVICE AGREEMENT DETAILS:

DETAILS & DATE OF REPAIRS: | DETAILS & DATE OF REPAIRS: | DETAILS & DATE OF REPAIRS:

ITEM: _____

MAKE/MODEL NO: _____

SERIAL NO: _____

DATE BOUGHT: _____

GUARANTEE EXPIRY DATE: _____

SERVICE AGREEMENT DETAILS: _____

_____

_____

DETAILS & DATE OF REPAIRS: _____

_____

_____

_____

_____

ITEM: _____

MAKE/MODEL NO: _____

SERIAL NO: _____

DATE BOUGHT: _____

GUARANTEE EXPIRY DATE: _____

SERVICE AGREEMENT DETAILS: _____

_____

_____

DETAILS & DATE OF REPAIRS: _____

_____

_____

_____

_____

ITEM: _____

MAKE/MODEL NO: _____

SERIAL NO: _____

DATE BOUGHT: _____

GUARANTEE EXPIRY DATE: _____

SERVICE AGREEMENT DETAILS: _____

_____

_____

DETAILS & DATE OF REPAIRS: _____

_____

_____

_____

_____

ITEM:

MAKE/MODEL NO:

SERIAL NO:

DATE BOUGHT:

GUARANTEE EXPIRY DATE:

SERVICE AGREEMENT DETAILS:

DETAILS & DATE OF REPAIRS:

ITEM:

MAKE/MODEL NO:

SERIAL NO:

DATE BOUGHT:

GUARANTEE EXPIRY DATE:

SERVICE AGREEMENT DETAILS:

DETAILS & DATE OF REPAIRS:

ITEM:

MAKE/MODEL NO:

SERIAL NO:

DATE BOUGHT:

GUARANTEE EXPIRY DATE:

SERVICE AGREEMENT DETAILS:

DETAILS & DATE OF REPAIRS:

ITEM:

MAKE/MODEL NO:

SERIAL NO:

DATE BOUGHT:

GUARANTEE EXPIRY DATE:

SERVICE AGREEMENT DETAILS:

DETAILS & DATE OF REPAIRS:

ITEM:

MAKE/MODEL NO:

SERIAL NO:

DATE BOUGHT:

GUARANTEE EXPIRY DATE:

SERVICE AGREEMENT DETAILS:

DETAILS & DATE OF REPAIRS:

ITEM:

MAKE/MODEL NO:

SERIAL NO:

DATE BOUGHT:

GUARANTEE EXPIRY DATE:

SERVICE AGREEMENT DETAILS:

ITEM: _____

_____

MAKE/MODEL NO: _____

SERIAL NO: _____

DATE BOUGHT: _____

GUARANTEE EXPIRY DATE: _____

SERVICE AGREEMENT DETAILS: ____

_____

_____

DETAILS & DATE OF REPAIRS: _____

_____

_____

_____

_____

_____

ITEM: _____

_____

MAKE/MODEL NO: _____

SERIAL NO: _____

DATE BOUGHT: _____

GUARANTEE EXPIRY DATE: _____

SERVICE AGREEMENT DETAILS: ____

_____

_____

DETAILS & DATE OF REPAIRS: _____

_____

_____

_____

_____

_____

ITEM: _____

_____

MAKE/MODEL NO: _____

SERIAL NO: _____

DATE BOUGHT: _____

GUARANTEE EXPIRY DATE: _____

SERVICE AGREEMENT DETAILS: ____

_____

_____

DETAILS & DATE OF REPAIRS: _____

_____

_____

_____

_____

_____

ITEM:

MAKE/MODEL NO:

SERIAL NO:

DATE BOUGHT:

ITEM:

MAKE/MODEL NO:

SERIAL NO:

DATE BOUGHT:

ITEM:

MAKE/MODEL NO:

SERIAL NO:

DATE BOUGHT:

ITEM:

MAKE/MODEL NO:

SERIAL NO:

DATE BOUGHT:

GUARANTEE EXPIRY DATE:

SERVICE AGREEMENT DETAILS:

DETAILS & DATE OF REPAIRS:

ITEM: ITEM: ITEM:

MAKE/MODEL NO: MAKE/MODEL NO: MAKE/MODEL NO:

SERIAL NO: SERIAL NO: SERIAL NO:

DATE BOUGHT: DATE BOUGHT: DATE BOUGHT:

GUARANTEE EXPIRY DATE: GUARANTEE EXPIRY DATE: GUARANTEE EXPIRY DATE:

SERVICE AGREEMENT DETAILS: SERVICE AGREEMENT DETAILS: SERVICE AGREEMENT DETAILS:

DETAILS & DATE OF REPAIRS: DETAILS & DATE OF REPAIRS: DETAILS & DATE OF REPAIRS:

Household Inventory

These pages enable you to list
all valuable items such as
paintings, gold and silverware,
and wrist watches. Together
with the serial numbers and
details on the Appliances pages
these would be invaluable in
compiling an insurance claim in
case of a fire or burglary.

Insurances

Use these pages to record details of all your insurance policies.
Policy numbers, payment details and details of cover can all be listed.
Here is a checklist of policies you may choose to list: car, health, home, house contents, life insurance, property (gold, paintings, silver, photographic equipment etc).

Don't forget to list all valuables under Household Inventory on page 26.

_____

_____

_____

_____

_____

_____

_____

_____

_____

_____

_____

_____

_____

_____

_____

_____

_____

_____

_____

_____

_____

_____

Finance

Enter details and policy numbers of investment policies, pension schemes, mortgages/rent and banking arrangements.
Telephone numbers, addresses and contact names can go in too.

Credit Card Records *Don't list your PIN numbers!*

List your credit charge and cash cards by type and number
and add the telephone number to ring if your card is lost or stolen.

CARD TYPE	CARD NUMBER	TELEPHONE

Decorations and Furnishing

Enter the item you want to record and add anything that will be vital in servicing, cleaning or tracing the supplier, or finding a matching replacement. Entering numbers and shade names for carpets and wallpaper will prove immensely helpful. Here is a checklist of items you may want to list: carpets, china, curtains, cutlery, linen, paints, tiles, towels and wallpaper.

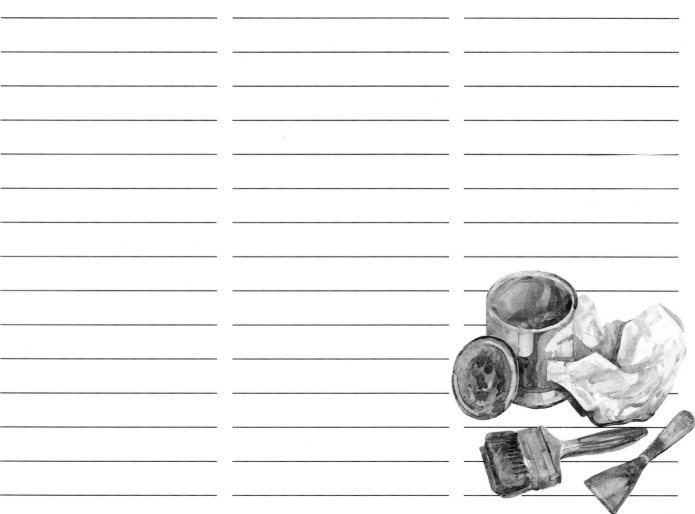

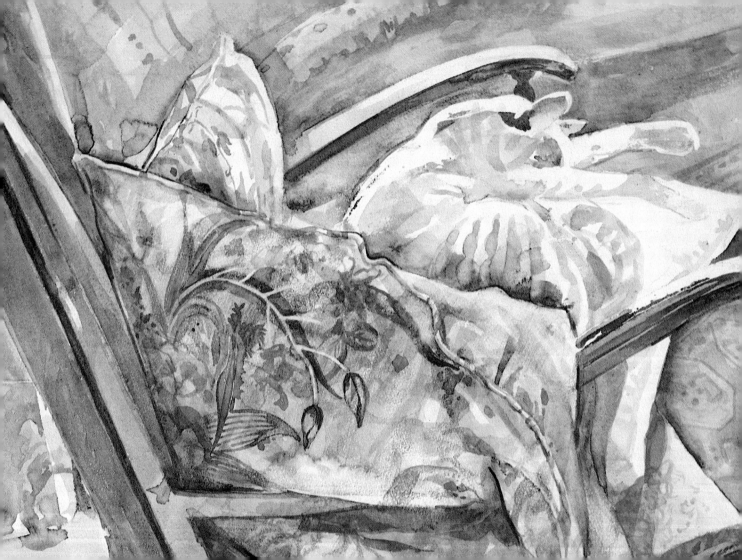

Directory

This is a section to record the names and addresses you need for your particular home. Every householder will choose differently and the lists of suggestions under the letters of the alphabet are just memory-joggers.

A

Accountant
Airport
Architect

_____

_____

_____

_____

_____

_____

_____

_____

_____

_____

_____

B

Babysitters
Bank
Book store
Bottle bank
Building society
Bus station

43

43

C

Car repairs
Car wash
Carpet cleaning service
Caterers
Cattery
Childsitter
Chimney sweep
Church
Cleaner
Clinic
Clubs
Coal merchant
Committees
Computer suppliers
Council offices
Crime Prevention Officer

D

Dairy
Dance teacher
Decorator
Delivery/courier services
Dentist
Dishwasher service
Doctor
Dry cleaner

E

Electrician
Electricity company
Emergency

49

F

Fast. food delivery
Fire station
Florist
Freezer food supplies
Freezer service

G

Garage
Garden supplies
Gardener
Gas company
Glazier
Gutter maintenance

H

Hairdresser
Hardware supplies
Health clinic
Heating engineer
Hospital
Hotels
Household waste
Housekeeper

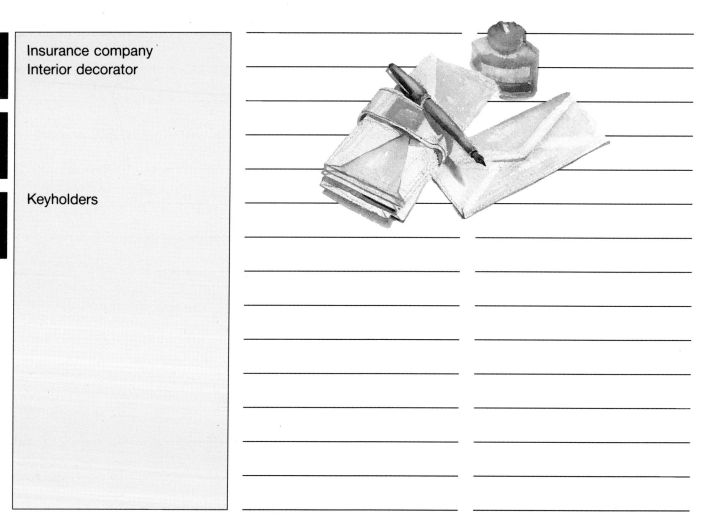

I Insurance company
Interior decorator

J

K Keyholders

L

Lawyer
Library
Locksmith

M

Microwave oven service
Motor organization
Music teacher

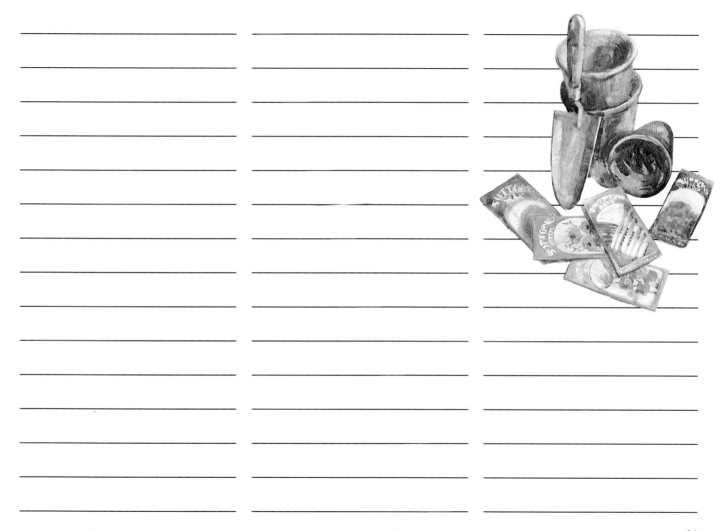

N

Newsagent
Nursery

O

Office
Oil supplier
Optician

P

Q

Painter
Parent/Teacher Association
Pension
Pizza delivery service
Plumber
Police Station
Post Office

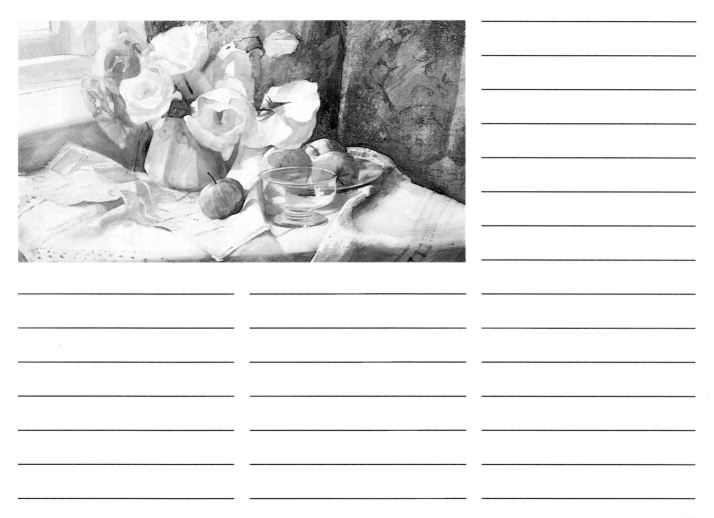

R

Railway station
Recycling services
Refrigerator service
Restaurants
Roof maintenance

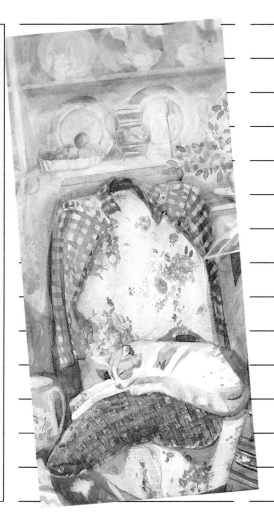

S

Schools
Security service
Sports clubs
Swimming pool

W
X
Y
Z

Washing machine service
Waste disposal
Water company
Window cleaner

Individual Personal Record

This page can be used for insurance numbers, personal assets, clothing sizes, work/school addresses and phone numbers, educational qualifications and passport number.

76

Health Record

Medical insurance details: Allergies, drugs taken, and other important medical information:

_____

_____

_____

_____

_____

_____

Blood group:

Childhood diseases

Give dates of vaccinations and estimated dates of any actual infections.
Combined vaccine
Measles _____
(recommended vaccination at 12 to 18 months)
Mumps _____
(recommended vaccination at 12 to 18 months)
Rubella _____
(recommended at 11 to 14 years – girls only)

Tetanus _____
Whooping Cough _____
Diphtheria _____
Polio _____
} 1st at 3 months 2nd at 5-6 months 3rd at 9-11 months

Immunizations for Travel

Cholera _____
(booster after six months)

Hepatitis A _____
(booster three to six months)

Hepatitis B _____
(booster three to five years)

Polio _____
(booster ten years)

Tetanus _____
(booster ten years)

Typhoid _____
(booster three years)

Yellow Fever _____
(booster ten years)

Individual Personal Record

NAME

This page can be used for insurance numbers, personal assets, clothing sizes, work/ school addresses and phone numbers, educational qualifications and passport number.

Health Record

Medical insurance details: Allergies, drugs taken, and other important medical information:

_____

_____

_____

_____

_____

Blood group:

Childhood diseases

Give dates of vaccinations and estimated dates of any actual infections.
Combined vaccine
Measles _____
(recommended vaccination at 12 to 18 months)
Mumps _____
(recommended vaccination at 12 to 18 months)
Rubella _____
(recommended at 11 to 14 years – girls only)

Tetanus _____
Whooping Cough _____
Diphtheria _____
Polio _____

} 1st at 3 months
2nd at 5-6 months
3rd at 9-11 months

Immunizations for Travel

Hepatitis B _____
(booster three to five years)

Typhoid _____
(booster three years)

Cholera _____
(booster after six months)

Polio _____
(booster ten years)

Yellow Fever _____
(booster ten years)

Hepatitis A _____
(booster three to six months)

Tetanus _____
(booster ten years)

Individual Personal Record

NAME _____

This page can be used for insurance numbers, personal assets, clothing sizes, work/ school addresses and phone numbers, educational qualifications and passport number.

Health Record

Medical insurance details: Allergies, drugs taken, and other important medical information:

_____

_____

_____

_____

_____

Blood group:

Childhood diseases

Give dates of vaccinations and estimated dates of any actual infections.
Combined vaccine
Measles _____
(recommended vaccination at 12 to 18 months)
Mumps _____
(recommended vaccination at 12 to 18 months)
Rubella _____
(recommended at 11 to 14 years – girls only)

Tetanus_____⎫ 1st at 3 months
Whooping Cough_____⎬ 2nd at 5-6 months
Diphtheria _____⎪ 3rd at 9-11 months
Polio_____⎭

Immunizations for Travel

Hepatitis B _____
(booster three to five years)

Typhoid _____
(booster three years)

Cholera _____
(booster after six months)

Polio _____
(booster ten years)

Yellow Fever _____
(booster ten years)

Hepatitis A_____
(booster three to six months)

Tetanus _____
(booster ten years)

Individual Personal Record

NAME

This page can be used for insurance numbers, personal assets, clothing sizes, work/ school addresses and phone numbers, educational qualifications and passport number.

Health Record

Medical insurance details: Allergies, drugs taken, and other important medical information:

_____

_____

_____

_____

_____

_____

Blood group:

Childhood diseases

Give dates of vaccinations and estimated dates of any actual infections.
Combined vaccine
Measles _____
(recommended vaccination at 12 to 18 months)
Mumps _____
(recommended vaccination at 12 to 18 months)
Rubella _____
(recommended at 11 to 14 years – girls only)

Tetanus _____
Whooping Cough _____
Diphtheria _____
Polio _____
} 1st at 3 months
2nd at 5-6 months
3rd at 9-11 months

Immunizations for Travel

Cholera _____
(booster after six months)

Hepatitis A _____
(booster three to six months)

Hepatitis B _____
(booster three to five years)

Polio _____
(booster ten years)

Tetanus _____
(booster ten years)

Typhoid _____
(booster three years)

Yellow Fever _____
(booster ten years)

Notes

If there are more than five
individuals in your household,
then these pages can be used for
extra personal individual
records. We've only provided
for four people, but there's
plenty of space here to add
many more.

In addition, you could use these
pages for records of pets, car
details, a Christmas card list, a
checklist of regular shopping or
a business/personal travel
packing checklist – or, any
hobby or special interest that
you need.

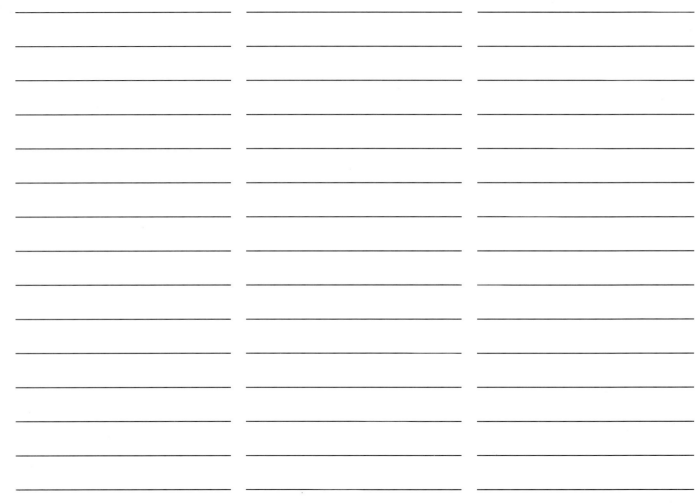

_____   _____   _____

_____   _____   _____

_____   _____   _____

_____   _____   _____

_____   _____   _____

_____   _____   _____

_____   _____   _____

_____   _____   _____